HAPPY LILY

ARYA PUNIA

BLUEROSE PUBLISHERS
India | U.K.

Copyright © Arya Punia 2024

All rights reserved by author. No part of this publication may be reproduced, stored in a retrieval system or transmitted in any form or by any means, electronic, mechanical, photocopying, recording or otherwise, without the prior permission of the author. Although every precaution has been taken to verify the accuracy of the information contained herein, the publisher assume no responsibility for any errors or omissions. No liability is assumed for damages that may result from the use of information contained within.

BlueRose Publishers takes no responsibility for any damages, losses, or liabilities that may arise from the use or misuse of the information, products, or services provided in this publication.

For permissions requests or inquiries regarding this publication, please contact:

BLUEROSE PUBLISHERS
www.BlueRoseONE.com
info@bluerosepublishers.com
+91 8882 898 898
+4407342408967

ISBN: 978-93-6452-987-7

First Edition: August 2024

Author and Illustrator Arya Punia

ABOUT THE BOOK

"The storybook follows Lily, a spirited 5-year-old who embarks on an exciting journey in a new country. Join Lily as she makes delightful new friends and learns valuable lessons from her adventures. Each story beautifully illustrates how she discovers the joy of friendship and the wisdom gained from her mistakes."

LONELY LILY

"One day, Lily was feeling very bored and lonely. She looked out of the window and felt sad because she had no friends. She decided to step out of the house and go for a walk. As Lily walked, she saw other kids playing together, which made her feel even sadder about not having a friend."

"It was very dark, so she decided to go back home. When she arrived, she went straight to her bedroom, fell asleep, and dreamed about her upcoming birthday.

Lily's birthday was in three days, and she couldn't wait for it."

The next morning, Lily woke up and went out for a walk. She saw a girl sitting alone in the park and found the perfect chance to make a friend. It was the first time Lily had ever tried to make a friend. She was very shy, but Lily did not give up.

Lily said, "Hi. What is your name?"

"My name is Diamond Tiara," the girl replied.

"What is your name?" Diamond Tiara asked.

"My name is Lily."

"How old are you?" Lily asked.

"I am 6 years old," Diamond Tiara replied.

"I am also 6 years old," Lily said happily.

Ice cream, ice cream, ice cream," said the ice cream man.

"Do you want some ice cream?" asked Diamond Tiara.

"Yes, of course. I would love to have some ice cream," Lily said.

"Which flavor do you want, Lily?" the ice cream man asked.

"I want orange flavor," Lily said.

Diamond Tiara said, "I want mango-flavored ice cream. And Lily, did you know my nickname is Diamond?"

"Oh! Nice I will call you Diamond from now on," Lily said.

"Lily, would you like to come to my play date?"

"Yes, I would love to come," Lily said.

Lily asked Diamond, "Will you come to my birthday party?"

Diamond said, "Yes, I would love to come. Thank you for the invite, Lily."

"Which cake will you have, Lily?"

"I don't know yet," Lily replied.

"It's very dark now. I think we should go home," Said Lily

"You are right, Lily," Diamond said.

"Bye, Lily. Bye, Diamond Tiara."

Lily went home and had her dinner. She was so happy that she had made a lovely friend. She slept peacefully.

FIRST SLEEPOVER

Ring, ring, ring, the telephone rang.

"Hello! Who is this?" Lily asked.

"It's me, Diamond, your friend."

"Oh! Hi, Diamond," Lily said.

Diamond asked, "Lily, do you want to come to my sleepover tomorrow?"

"Yes, I would love to come," Lily replied with excitement.

"Bye, Lily."

"Bye, Diamond."

The next morning, Lily woke up, ate her breakfast, and got ready to go to her friend's house.

"Lily was so excited for her first sleepover. She arrived at her friend's house and started playing with her friend.

After playing a lot of games, Lily and her friend decided to watch a movie.

'Which movie do you want to see?' asked Diamond.

'Trolls,' said Lily.

'Okay, then let's watch it. 'said Diamond.

They started enjoying the movie with popcorn and ice cream.

After some time, they began feeling sleepy, so they turned off the television and went to bed.

In the middle of the night, Lily started crying. Diamond woke up and asked, "Lily, what happened?"

Lily said, "I am missing my mother." Diamond gave her an idea to do a video call to her mom from her mother's phone.

After making a video call to her mother, Lily was happy and relaxed.

Diamond became so happy to see her friend smiling. They said good night to each other and fell asleep.

TOOTH PAIN

One day, Lily woke up early in the morning and saw that her mom and dad were still sleeping. Lily was very hungry, so she went into the kitchen to find something to eat. She saw chocolate spread jar.

She was so happy. She could not control and started eating chocolate spread with the spoon.

Then she heard some noise, she thought her mother woke up and coming in the kitchen.

She got scared that her mother will scold her for eating chocolate spread with spoon. So, she closed the jar and ran to her room then she realized that her mother did not notice that she had chocolate spread.

So now whenever her mother was not around she would go to the kitchen and eats one spoon full of chocolate spread and sweets

One day her tooth started paining and Lily started crying. Lily's mother got worried and took her to the dentist.

Dentist fixed her tooth problem but Lily had to go through lot of pain during the treatment.

After the treatment, dentist told Lily not to eat so much of sweets and brush teeth twice a day.

After listening to the doctor's advice Lily felt bad. She realized her mistake and she told to her mother that she was eating a lot of sweets and chocolate spread without telling her.

Lily was scared of telling the truth to her mother. After knowing Lily's mistake her mother gave her tight hug and told her that she is happy that she learnt from her mistake.

Lily become happy and made a promise that she will look after her teeth and never hide anything from her.

Lily went home happily.

FIRST DAY OF SCHOOL

Lily was so excited to go to school. When Lily reached school she started enjoying in school with her new friends.

When she was having lunch during recess her classmate Cayde came to her and started bullying her.

Lily felt terrible and started to cry, but her new friends made her feel better.

Next day when lily went to school Cayde bullied her again and Lily felt bad again. She went home and told her mother about Cayde behavior.

Lily's mother told her if she bully's you next time tell her you don't like it and please be kind with me.

Next day at school Cayde again bullied Lily.

Lily told her exactly what her mother told her to do but Cayde did listen to her and made fun of her.

When she went home she told everything to her mother and her mother told her to ignore her but kind always.

One day during recess Cayde accidentally dropped her lunch box.

Lily saw her crying and she felt bad that she has nothing to eat now so lily offered her lunch to Cayde.

When Cayde saw Lily's kindness, she felt ashamed on her behavior and said sorry to Lily. Lily forgives her and they become friends.

ABOUT THE AUTHOR

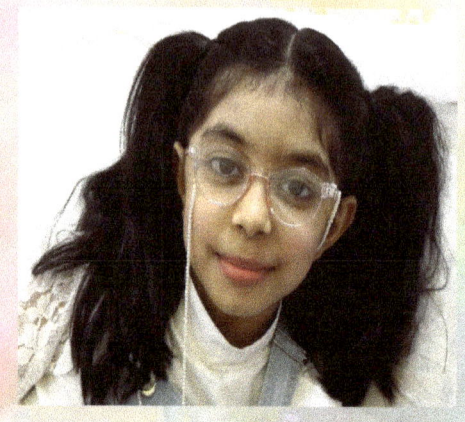

Meet Arya Punia, a creative 6-year-old born in 2017 in Aberdeen, Scotland. Arya's passion for storytelling shines through in her debut book, "Happy Lily." Having lived overseas in countries like Scotland and Kazakhstan, Arya adores exploring new places and discovering new things, which inspires her imaginative tales. Her joyous spirit extends to making friends wherever she goes, embodying the kindness and curiosity that define her. In her free time, Arya indulges in dancing, singing, and diving into captivating books, reflecting her vibrant personality and boundless imagination.

Share your feedback about the story book at itsmamtapunia@gmail.com

www.ingramcontent.com/pod-product-compliance
Lightning Source LLC
LaVergne TN
LVHW061627070526
838199LV00070B/6615